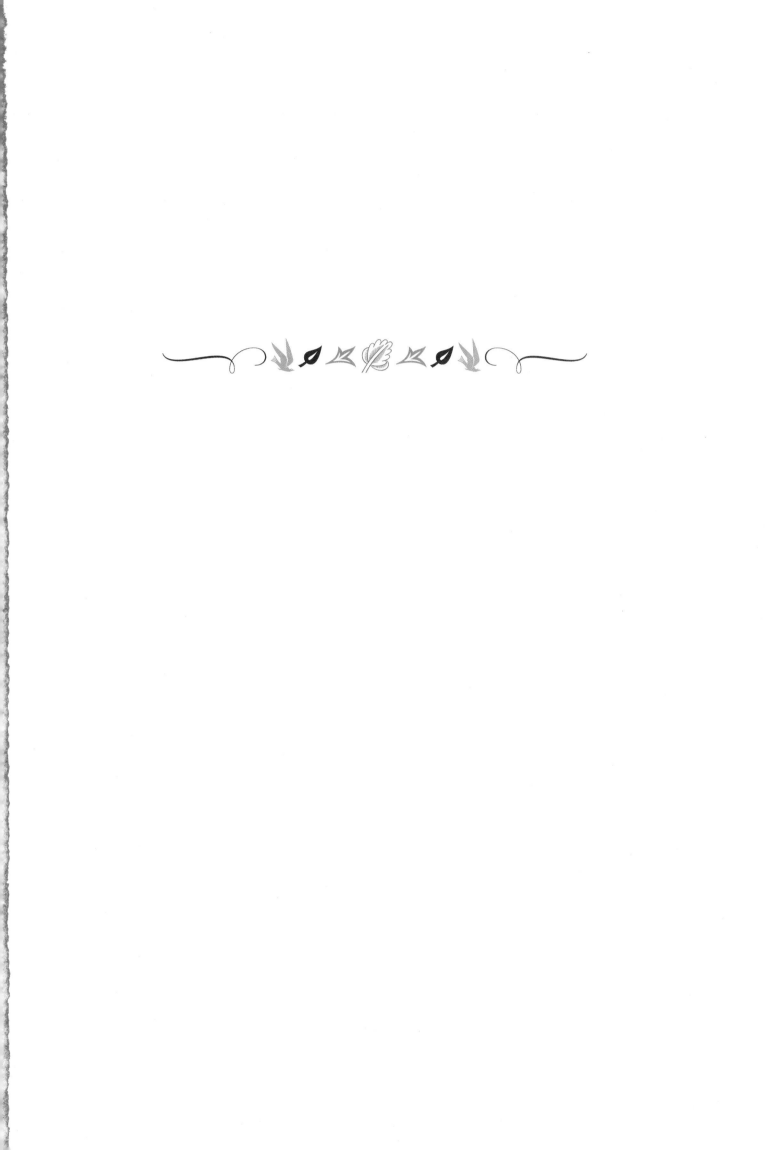

Text copyright © 2015 by Jane Yolen

Illustrations copyright © 2015 by Lisel Jane Ashlock

Published in 2015 by Creative Editions. P.O. Box 227, Mankato, MN 56002 USA

Creative Editions is an imprint of The Creative Company   www.thecreativecompany.us

All rights reserved. No part of the contents of this book may be reproduced by

any means without the written permission of the publisher. Printed in China

Library of Congress Cataloging-in-Publication Data Yolen, Jane.

Sing a season song / by Jane Yolen; illustrated by Lisel Jane Ashlock.

Summary: Illustrations and rhyming text introduce the four seasons

as icicle popsicles drip, daffodils bloom on hills, fireflies blink on and off,

and honking geese fly by. ISBN 978-1-56846-255-4

[1. Stories in rhyme. 2. Seasons—Fiction.]

I. Ashlock, Lisel Jane, illustrator. II. Title.

PZ8.3.Y76Shm 2015   [E]—dc23   2014022593

9 8 7 6 5 4 3

Written by **Jane Yolen**

SING A
SEASON
SONG

Illustrated by **Lisel Jane Ashlock**

Designed by Rita Marshall

Creative Editions

✳ Snow, snow,
shiver and blow.
Icicle popsicles
drip, drop, and dropsicles.

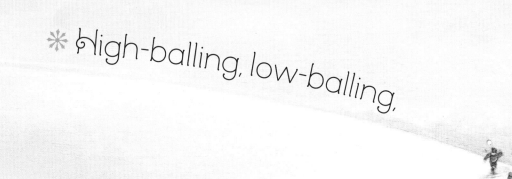

✳ High-balling, low-balling,

everyone's snowballing,

and it keeps going

on snowing.

✳ Snow flakes on snow cakes
and pictures the frost makes.

✳ Fingers and toes freeze
and cold makes my nose sneeze.
Turn the heat on,
  then winter is gone.

Frogs, trees,
hum-bumble bees,
blossoms and possums
and gossamer breeze.

Daffodils
on the hills,
pillows of lawn.

First rabbit,

first robin,

first baby fawn.

Then springtime is gone.

Water, waves,
shimmering days.
Toes wiggle,

fish wriggle

in a strange haze.

Run over,
turn over.
Day shines at night

Winking out,

blinking out,

firefly light:

off-again-on.

　　Then summer is gone.

Leaf.
Leaves
drifting from trees.

Capture
and keep them,
fling them
and heap them.

Pumpkins and gourds
and the clamor
of herds.
Honking geese Vs.
And the bare-bones of trees.

The very first freeze
making berry-red knees.
Late, later dawn.
    Then autumn is gone.

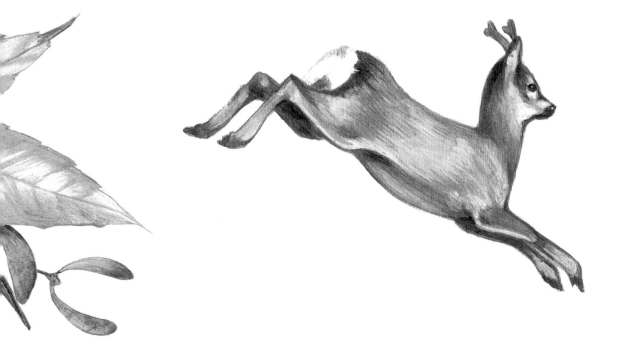

Round we all go . . .
shiver and blow . . .
and here, once again,
comes the snow.